You Shou

FOOD TRUCK

How to Start, Run, and Grow a Successful Food Truck Business on a Budget

By

Jackee Wilson-Moore

Published by:

Streets of Dream
Press

Streets of Dream Press

Cover & Interior designed

By

Renee Leadsman

First Edition

Contents

Introduction

My coworkers always accused me of over-sensationalizing any story. They would let out a huge sigh before I would begin to recount the highlights of a prior event that occurred. Even the ones handed down to me by my elders that carried traces of mythology oftentimes fell on deaf ears.

In fact, when I spoke of the woman in my picture album who carried chicken on the top of her head, they laughed in utter disbelief. I had merely scratched the surface on the history behind this striking-looking female handing food to the passengers on a railroad train. It wasn't hard to make the connection between my cooking skills and this unknown female who stood out amongst the other women in the yellowing photographs in the family photo album.

She was part of the chicken vendors in the 1800s who were part of the newly emancipated slaves who seized the opportunity in marketing and selling their fried foods to the soldiers and tourists on holiday during the Civil War. Apparently, the best cooks would earn the most money from those riders who took the train that made its now historic scheduled stop in the town of Gordonsville, Virginia. So, I'm told, these events put this previously obscure town on the map.

This location became known as the "Fried Chicken Capital of the World," according to historians and local townspeople who crafted their own versions of this tale. The Virginia Central Railroad and the Alexandria Railroad had carried thousands of Confederate and Union soldiers on the trail. After the Civil War, the railroad had stood center stage of Gordonsville's rich legacy. The city continued to be a rail stop even after the Chesapeake and Ohio Railroad took over ownership.

These entrepreneurial women called "waiter carriers" paved a way to financial stability with fried chicken in the 1800s. This is why Gordonsville stands out as the "Fried Chicken

Capital." Railroad trains did not have dining cars during this period, and these African American women capitalized on this opportunity providing homemade fried chicken, biscuits, and pies. The women would balance platters on their heads to serve the passengers through open railcar windows.

This practice became very popular, where passengers would reroute their trips purposely for the waiter carriers. These waiter carriers obtained economic empowerment at this critical period after the War. During the latter part of the 1900s, government regulations shut down track-side vendors, which resulted in the dissolution of the practice. This legacy is commemorated in Gordonsville with a yearly fried chicken contest.

As the story goes, the county's first African American women entrepreneurs earned gainful employment through handing platters of chicken through open railcar windows as these passengers passed through, carrying baskets of homemade poultry. Even after 1914, when the trains began to use dining cars, these women or descendants would allow conductors to pick up the ready-made chicken.

A thing of the past, Gordonsville's residents decided to commemorate this rich legacy by holding an annual festival in its honor with cooking contests, cash prizes, and bragging rights. This event is held at the Gordonsville fairgrounds' Fire

Department and wine garden along with a dessert contest, arts and crafts vendors, and bouncy houses for the kids, and live entertainment. There is also a Civil War Museum that once served as a place for wounded soldiers and later a hospital for slaves.

I decided to embrace my heritage and advertise my personal history with my food truck as the great-granddaughter of one of these fried chicken vendors in the late seventeenth century. Customers would surely gravitate to the business with such an engaging history. This would be my niche or my selling card to separate me from my competition and drive sales.

My food truck would be located in Gordonsville at that exact spot. Additionally, according to the Virginia Tourism Corporation and the Travel Association, Orange County, where Gordonsville is located, exceeds $51 million in tourism revenue annually. There are a few reasons which can account for this growing economic market.

Contrary to some future entrepreneurs, I didn't have an "ah-ha" moment in planning to start a food truck business. The idea actually began through my own reflection of my life.

It was clear that the 9-5 job wasn't going to cut it. After payday, I barely had enough money left over for gas to get to work after my expenses. Basically, every week, my co-worker glamourized business ideas she presented to me in different ways to earn more dispensable cash. She was also known for being all talk and no follow-through.

I, on the other hand, was quite the opposite. I believed in digging my heels in to accomplish my goal. I had a running start over the competition of an already vetted audience. I loved to cook! I was already cooking for an audience.

People from far and wide would line up to taste the delicious meals I'd prepared on weekends and after work. I even took orders from them for special occasions like weddings, birthdays, and anniversaries. I already had a ready-made audience for my offerings. I decided to take one of my co-worker's seemingly "hair-brained" schemes and bring it to life - starting a food truck!

Getting down to the basics of how to start a food truck business led me to research everything on the subject. This book contains everything I found out, from my initial research to my own experience running my food truck.

Chapter 1: Planning

Basically, a food truck is a huge motorized vehicle, like a portable restaurant of sorts where food is prepared and served for a cost. A few of these enterprises serve items like ice cream, French fries, hamburgers, ethnic foods, gourmet meals, and other made-to-order selections. Often these foods are prepared in an off-site kitchen, frozen, and served hot at the designated location. These mobile-style eateries have gained popularity over the course of several years.

A History of Food Trucks

The chuckwagon was a form of a food truck that came along way before the mobile food truck came into existence. The chuckwagon dates all the way back to the early 1800s. For the most part, the chuckwagon was used to transport cattle and cooking equipment to customers in America and Canada.

The lunch wagon came about by Walter Scott in 1872 when he created a small cart to sell sandwiches, coffee, and desserts to customers at a local paper company.

Years later, the wagon would evolve into canteens used by the U.S. Army serving military personnel wherever they were stationed.

Pros and Cons

I made a list to weigh the pros and cons of my mobile unit versus starting a full-scale food truck. At the top of my list was the revelation that food trucks, food carts, and food booths stood at the forefront of the street vendors industry, which accounted for nearly $2 million in customers on a daily basis.

The biggest advantage or pros of a mobile food truck versus a traditional eat-in food truck is its ability to go where the customers are at any particular time. This could be a busy area where there is a lot of traffic to help generate additional capital on a weekly basis.

Other benefits to a mobile food truck are that the cost to operate pales in comparison to the expense of a fully-operational kitchen-type food truck.

The cons of such an enterprise are that it is usually seasonal. It requires long working hours for the first several years, even in bad weather.

Initial Considerations

I would call my mobile venture a nourishment truck. This should surely appeal to the health-conscious customer. These days, there's an entire movement surrounding eating healthy meals instead of fatty junk food when you're in a hurry.

I decided that I could hitch a trailer to a truck full of prepared menu items and serve them. If I could find a mobile vehicle with a kitchen, I would make good use of it by expanding the food choices.

Once I had gathered enough information on the projected establishment, or adequate research that could give me a running start on the business, I could settle myself and feel secure my dream of owning a mobile food truck was within my reach.

This is the thing I discovered in gathering food truck resources is that two heads are better than one. Pulling from the expertise of others is a sure-fire strategy to claim my victory with this endeavor.

location. location. location

One of the most important aspects of starting a mobile food enterprise is to choose an area to station your truck. Every city or town will have regulations regarding your operation. When you have picked out a suitable location, check with the place on what the laws or ordinances are related to how to park your food truck there legally.

Costs

Food trucks are expensive to purchase and could take a large chuck out of your initial start-up costs. To purchase a new pull behind style trailer truck, it is estimated that you might spend $15,000. I had heard this figure from some vendors with similar operations. The option to build your truck from the ground up may save money in the long run. This would mean contracting out labor to bring the mobile unit up to code and buying the necessary equipment since it isn't already installed.

Unless you have saved up a lot of money or have cash lying around, you will need to seek financing. Try local community banks, business bureaus, or angels (personal investors) to provide the upfront money. Include operation costs, any maintenance on the vehicle, marketing, food expenses, and licensing regulations.

The largest part of your startup budget will be the food truck itself. Be sure to select one capable of performing well for you. The important aspects to consider are noted below whether you decide to lease or buy the vehicle used or spanking brand new:

Do your homework. Select a food truck seller that is reputable and has a good review from previous customers who have done business with them. Determine what customization required for your food truck.

Obtain insurance right away for your truck and business generally to protect against unforeseen events. Ensure that inspections and permits are satisfied, and your truck is operating legally.

Permits and licensing

Health and safety requirements may involve other necessary permits and licensing. You have to keep up with the appearance of your truck like lighting, painting, outside menus, cooking equipment, oil changes, oil, tires, and other maintenance at some point. An inspector will instruct you on what the requirements are for operating a food truck in serving the general public.

Once you decide on a location, you will need to apply for whatever licenses and permits that are required for that particular locale. Sometimes, this may involve a long waiting period to gain approval. Permits sometimes require annual renewals for food truck business owners.

Consider Technology

Stay up to date with technological advances. Social media has shown signs of improving the bottom line for business owners across the board and regardless of industry. Post information on a daily basis or as often as possible to social media channels like Facebook, Twitter, and Instagram to promote and market your businesses and engage customers.

Owning your own business is hard work. You will find yourself wearing many hats from dishwasher, cashier, cook, customer service representative, bookkeeper, and accountant.

Consider as best you can what's actually involved in owning and operating your own food truck business.

Deciding on food

Your menu defines you. The food you choose to serve will need to be according to the theme or niche that you set.

You don't want to start out as a vegan food truck, but then abruptly decide that pork dishes would be cheaper to source and change your food idea midstream. Pick a niche (your food) and stick with it. You will want to fill a need in the community with your food offerings. Is your area lacking in a particular cuisine type, not just in food trucks but in the area food trucks as well? Find that hole to fill.

You will also want to think about how much it costs to create your menu. We will talk about this in-depth later. In general, the food you offer will determine what equipment you need and how many people you need to assist you in making it.

Chapter 2: Financing

It's not a good idea to perform any task on a wing and prayer.

Meaning, consider all aspects of a function or action before diving right in.

Think clearly about the best and the worst scenarios with all future projections.

I say "projections," because you're basing your next step on a plan that hasn't happened yet without any prior experience to draw on. This couldn't be clearer than when money is involved.

Let me say at the outset that I am, by nature a risk-taker. Yet, before I make a move on winning, the odds are stacked against them in my favor. In the case of acquiring a food truck, particularly, think about some of the advantages of purchasing the vehicle outright versus renting the mobile unit until you get up and running and earning a stable profit. Buying a truck is quite a sizeable financial outlay of cash.

You should know your market, the economic climate, competition activities, and a willingness to commit to growing this business aggressively for the next five to ten years.

Seasoned experts in the food truck industry suggest a new owner should rent the vehicle first to test out the idea. See if there is enough income to be made and if it is something that you are actually committed to seeing through to the end. For instance, the cost of a six-month lease can range anywhere from $2K to $3K a month, generally speaking.

When negotiating the contract with the rental companies, find out which party is responsible for insurance, maintenance, permits, utilities, cleaning, and any other required permits.

There are several financing options available to help finance your food truck on wheels.

1.Small business loans are for those entrepreneurs-to-be seeking money for equipment, inventory, working capital, or other fixed assets. These types of loans may require some collateral as a personal guaranty from the owner. Repayment of these loans is usually stretched out for three to ten years or six to 12 months in the shorter term. This loan is best for one-time items such as to purchase equipment or machinery.

2. Small Business Administration (SBA) loans are monies the government guarantees. This is best for capital needed over a long period of time. The application process can be exhaustive but fully worth going the extra mile. They are obtained through a bank with an SBA loan program. However, these loans could require stronger credit scores and upfront fees.

The SBA microloan program offers business loans as much as $50,000, which are generated by third-party lenders. These are typically obtained from network agencies trying to lend to organizations in order to make a local impact. SBA-backed microloans are used to buy elements, fixtures, machinery, or to cover operating capital expenses. Repayment terms are typically up to 6 years, with interest charges between 8-13%.

3. A business line of credit is usually based on accounts receivables as well as inventory as collateral and offer more flexibility to repay. Some of these loans require a personal guarantee. Higher fees may be required. Business owners typically use these monies for unexpected expenses, cash flow needs, and managing their working capital.

A business line of credit could let you withdraw funds to pay for enterprise fees, which includes kitchen supplies and substances, on an as-needed basis. When you pay off what you borrow, your complete credit limit will become available again. You'll only pay interest on what you borrow, even though your interest rate may be higher based on your credit score history.

4. Invoice factoring is a type of loan where a business owner can use unpaid invoices into cash for the use of a factoring company. The factoring company does all the collecting from your customers and then distributes it to your company for a designated fee.

5. Angel investors/venture capital are funders who usually lend money in exchange for some form of ownership in a business.

6. Equipment financing can be used to buy commercial business property, which includes ovens and cooking components. This system acts as collateral for the loan, making it less volatile for the lender and more on hand for the commercial enterprise owner. But most lenders would require you to make a down payment of 10-20%, which could be a large amount in case you're financing other costly equipment. You may also use an equipment loan to buy the food truck itself. In that case, the vehicle might secure the mortgage.

7. You could use a short-term loan to cover any food truck costs, probably paying off your debt in 3 to 18 months. Short-term loans generally come in smaller amounts and can have excessive interest rates, depending on the length of your reimbursement terms, your enterprise's cash flow, your credit rating, and your overall risk as a borrower.

8. Microloans that are dispensed in small amounts as much as $50,000 offer operating capital to cover commercial enterprise charges, consisting of stock, resources, or equipment. Microloans are tied to community improvement initiatives and are typically issued to certain kinds of

commercial enterprise proprietors — including minorities, females, veterans, or not-for-profit organizations, depending on the lender. Collateral is required.

9. Credibly is an online alternative commercial lender offering flexible, short-term funding to small commercial enterprise owners. Its working capital loan is available to business proprietors with a FICO score of 500 or higher, six months in business, and $15,000 or extra in normal monthly deposits at the bank.

Qualified applicants may borrow as much as $400,000 for 6 to 18 months. Credibly makes use of current market rates to determine interest on loans, and you'll need to multiply your interest fee with your loan amount to calculate the overall balance, which you might owe. It advertises going rates as low as 1.15. Payments could coordinate with a daily or weekly timetable. You may receive funds as quickly as the next day, to cover any business expense.

10. Online lender Kabbage offers enterprise lines of credit as much as $250,000 for certified borrowers at APRs around 8.00% – 24.00%. To qualify, you want to be in business for at least 12 months with $50,000 in annual revenue or $4,200 in month-to-month income throughout the past 3 months. In every instance where you draw from your line of credit, you'll have 6 or 18 months to pay back the amount you borrowed.

11. Food truck proprietors who use PayPal to accept bills simply should take benefit of PayPal's working capital, a loan program that allows you to borrow cash primarily based on your income. You could borrow as much as 35% of your annual PayPal income and no more than $125,000 on your first loan. To acquire payments, PayPal might take a percentage of every sale you are making through its platform.

12. Crest Capital is an online lender that gives equipment financing as much as $250,000 for eligible small business owners. You can finance the total value of the machinery or used device to get an equipment lease. Repayment terms range from 24 to 72 months. Your industry, time in business, business credit records, and equipment type may influence your eligibility.

Crest Capital ranks on the top for its pricing alternatives and a huge variety of repayment and food truck financing options, as well as its impeccable online popularity. To apply for an equipment loan or rent with Crest Capital, borrowers can fill out an application on-line for same-day approvals and apply for the most suitable leases to up to $250,000.

Crest Capital is mainly an equipment leasing provider with flexible terms that can cover your food truck financing needs. There's also 100% financing available as much as $500,000 on a wide variety of packages for new and used equipment. With over 30 years of experience in leasing, Crest Capital combines two types of leasing--automobiles title loans and equipment, all under one roof.

How Much?

Most foodies who work in the industry see signs of 7% or more growth over the first five years in the mobile truck industry. Oftentimes, the food truck business is a better investment than an all-out food truck, but you may need to secure financing to stay rolling.

You could easily start a food truck company for around $200,000 compared to opening an eatery for over $1million. Used stand-alone full-service food trucks run around $40,000 to $80,000. The legal requirements such as permits, licenses, and health certificates are an estimated cost of $28,000.

Inventory to cook and serve the meals can exceed $1,000, according to the U.S. Chamber of Commerce Foundation. But there is a silver lining when you cannot cover all the costs of the venture using your own money. There are financing options available. Charges can easily stack up when you start a food truck commercial enterprise. This will consist of supplies and equipment. While you begin a food truck business, fees can also pile up quickly. From kitchen components and ingredients to gas and automobile maintenance, the cost of running the business may also exceed the money in your bank account.

Financing from small business lenders allows you to maintain the operation of your food truck. Whether or not you're taking out a short-term food truck loan or line of credit to cover widespread charges, or equipment financing to pay for objects, the variety of finance options allow you to cover monetary gaps within the business.

Keep in mind to maintain your business costs low, which includes incorporating flexible and seasonal items on your menu and staying away from overspending on groceries. You could also buy inventory in bulk with other food truck owners in your area to bring down costs. In a few cases, it could be less expensive to lease equipment or buy used equipment and machinery instead of buying a new property.

Chapter 3: Licensing

Food truck businesses require numerous licenses and permits to function. These licenses and permits should be received before you open for business. The food truck licenses and permits you'll want for your food truck business vary for each town, county, and country.

Please note that a few regions can also require you to sign up your enterprise yearly, gathering a fee whenever you have to renew. To discover what you need for the region your business will be positioned in, communicate with your county or city clerk. The subsequent lists reveal the most required food truck licenses and permits. Here are the standard requirements for food truck licenses and permits.

Employer Identification Number

Food trucks generally require numerous employees. To function within the regulations, you want an employer identification number (EIN). An EIN is utilized by the IRS to become aware of your enterprise and acquire taxes from you, and employees. You could apply free to your state EIN through eFax or online by visiting the IRS internet site.

Business license

Each food truck business needs to obtain a business license to operate. Depending on the city and state, you will be charged a percent of your gross sales or once a year fee, alongside the license fee.

Please note: The food truck licenses stipulation of any area are subject to change so that you may also need to sign up for your nearby food truck or food truck affiliation to stay-up to date on any modifications in laws.

Automobile license

Due to the fact that your enterprise is on wheels, you'll need to ensure the truck itself, and its drivers are certified. Depending on the weight of the automobile, certain states may also require a business driver's license to operate your food truck.

In some states, food truck proprietors need to use an assigned supplier so you can purchase food and different goods at wholesale prices without paying sales tax.

Food Handler's Permit

Some cities and states require one or more personnel of a food truck to have a food handler's permit. The city or state may also require additional personnel to take a food safety class before the permit is issued.

Protect your food truck business. Make sure you've got a person with a legitimate food handler's permit to operate the track during open business hours.

Health Department Permit

Your food truck, like any food truck, needs to be inspected through the health department. Your meal truck (and commissary) may also need to as well. The evaluation and approval from your local health department will confirm that the food you put together is being maintained and created in a safe way.

fire Certificate

The fire department will certainly check out your food truck in case you're using cooking equipment on board. They'll train you on the regulations you need to comply with, and that they'll do recurring inspections on your food truck fire suppression system.

The bottom line is it is essential to satisfy all the regulatory requirements on your food truck. This can assist you in avoiding expensive fines and possible enterprise closure. Every town, county, and state has its very own food truck licensing and requirements. Providers can look for the specific business license and requirements in their area on the U.S. Small Business Administration website.

Types of Regulations You May Encounter

This data doesn't cover every health guideline or rule but does give you a general feel for guiding you in the right direction in terms of foundational laws. Take a moment to analyze these facts and figures, and it will hopefully expedite your foodservice application.

The following list includes the requirements and regulations that I had to adhere to while running my food truck business in Virginia.

Mobile food license

A mobile food business license is permitted and evaluated on a yearly basis, allowing permission for county or city health departments in the Commonwealth of Virginia to inspect performance on an everyday basis. Mobile units are confined to a certain allowed distance from its normal base of operations, returning to the service area at least once a day.

Event Permits

A temporary event permit is granted for one occasion with no more than 14 consecutive days permission granted to provide meals on a temporary basis. Meal service centers constructed for providing meals on a temporary basis are to be issued via the temporary/unique occasion.

legalese

These are the definitions from the Commonwealth of Virginia's handbook on the laws governing food truck operations.

Accepted Water Supply - A water source which ▚
legitimate waterworks operation permit from the heal▚
department or a nonpublic water supply that's evaluated,
examined, and is found in affordable compliance with
production standards of the private properly rules and the
bacteriological water requirements of the Virginia
Waterworks rules, accepted and permitted via the health
branch director or designee. Periodic water checks can be
required for personal water materials.

Commissary - A catering establishment, food truck, or
another area wherein food, food containers, or materials are
stored, treated, prepared, packaged, or stored for distribution
to satellite operations.

Effortlessly-cleanable - A characteristic of a floor that: (a)
permits powerful elimination of soil through regular cleaning
techniques; (b) Is depending on the material, layout,
creation, and installation of the surface; and (c) Varies with
the chance of the surface's position in introducing
pathogenic or toxigenic dealers or different contaminants
into food primarily based at the surface's permitted
placement, reason, and use. ·

Mobile food unit – A meal establishment that is set up on
wheels that is effortlessly portable from place to place and
encompasses pushcarts, trailers, trucks, or vans. There's no

obile devices; however, they need to be
ughout its operation and must be on
ception of boats within the water) always.
tions, and all equipment need to be crucial
r attached to the unit.

Packaged - Cartoned, securely bagged, bottled, canned, or
wrapped securely, whether or not packaged in a food
processing plant or a food establishment.

Person-In-charge - The person present on the food
establishment who's liable for the operation at the time of
inspection.

Pushcart – Any wheeled automobile or device apart from a
motor automobile or trailer, which can be moved without or
with the help of a motor and which does not require
registration through the Department of Motor vehicles. A
pushcart is restricted to the sale and/or service of hot dogs
and frankfurter-like foods. The unit, all onsite operations, and
all equipment need to be essential to and be inside or
attached to the unit. A pushcart calls for a commissary
where wares may be washed, wastewater may be
discharged, and in which food, supplies, and the unit can be
stored when not in operation.

Servicing region – A running base area to which a mobile food establishment or transportation automobile frequently returns for things like vehicle and device cleaning, discharging liquid or strong wastes, refilling water tanks and ice bins, and boarding food.

Sewage – Liquid waste containing animal or vegetable matter in suspension or answer and can consist of water containing chemical compounds in solution.

Temporary food establishment – A food establishment that operates for a duration of no greater than 14 consecutive days alongside a single occasion or celebration

Tie/Temperature control for safety (TCS) food- a food that calls for time and/or temperature control so that you can restrict pathogenic microorganism bloom or toxin formation.

Best Practices

All openings to the outside need to be screened or equipped with different devices to repel or prevent the entrance of flies, bugs, and vermin (besides when foods are being served via a service window).

Production substances and all surfaces need to be clean, non-absorbent, and effortlessly washable, ideally which encompasses clean material which includes chrome steel or plastic.

All mobile units have to offer the right system for foods on the menu. Every mobile unit or pushcart in which unpackaged food is handled needs to have a handwashing sink with hot and cold water, distributed soap, paper towels, and a wastebasket. This is a must for all devices besides those serving best-prepackaged foods and bottled beverages.

A three-compartment sink is needed. It needs to be massive enough to deal with the immersion of most devices and utensils. It needs to have drainboards, utensil racks, or tables big enough to deal with utensil maintenance before cleaning and after sanitizing and accommodate all dirty and cleaning gadgets that can collect at some point in the hours of operation.

A potable and wastewater tank is needed for all units, aside from those serving prepackaged goods. The quantity of the wastewater tank should be 15 % larger than the quantity of potable water storage tanks. Refrigeration is needed that is able to keep temperature control for the protection of food. All food and ice need to be bought from a permitted source.

Home-canned or home-prepared foods aren't allowed to be stored on the unit or served to the general public. No food made in a personal home can be used, stored, served, and provided for sale, offered, or given away in a food facility.

A food thermometer should be available and used to test internal food temperatures. Condiments, which include sugar, ketchup, mustard, salt, and mayonnaise, need to be covered from contamination through being kept in dispensers which are designed to offer safety.

Chapter 4: food Safety Guidelines

Every establishment that deals in the preparation and distribution of food has to follow appropriate safety standards. Here are some important tips to follow.

Storage and Cleanliness

Foods that have been cooked and/or heated can't be cooled and reused until the operator can show that such cooling may be accomplished in line with the subsequent guidelines:

Cooked food should be cooled:

1. Inside two hours, from 1350 f (570 c) to 700 f (210 c)

2. Inside 4 hours, from 700 f (210 c) to 410 f (50 c) or less. Meals need to be cooled inside 4 hrs. to 41 f (50 c) or less if organized from elements at required temperatures, which includes foods and tuna canned.

Raw shell eggs need to be straight away positioned in a refrigeration device that keeps an ambient air temperature of 450 f (70 c) or less.

Onboard storage needs to be restricted to objects essential for operation. Food storage boxes need to be food grade.

All water needs to be potable, from a permitted supply. The mobile unit can also connect with water and sewer if it is available on the operating location, but the tank needs to continue to be at the unit always. Ice to be used as a food or a cooling medium have to be crafted from consuming water. Ice for human intake needs to be included, drained, and stored separately from ice used for refrigeration. Ice needs to be distributed using an ice scoop.

All wastewater needs to be disposed of in a business facility (commissary or carrier area).

Wiping cloths used for wiping down countertops need to be clean, used for no different reason, and stored in a container with sanitizer (I.E., Chlorine or quaternary ammonium).

An employee health policy is required. The manager should make sure all employees are knowledgeable about the necessary procedures if they're inflamed with a communicable infection, diarrhea, have had vomiting, sore throat with fever, and/or jaundice in the past 48 hours. This person should have the authority to send a worker home.

Every operator, worker, or volunteer needs to be clean with clean clothing and put on effective hair restraints (hair nets, caps, and so on.).

No bare hand contact is permitted with food. Suitable barriers include tongs, scoops, disposable gloves, and deli tissue/paper.

Food provider workers need to wash hands when starting to work, between converting duties, after working with raw meat, and any time their hands also have been infected with body fluids or different kinds of contaminants such as, after smoking, consuming food, or using the restroom.

Every Food Truck is Required to Have a Commissary

There are basically two types of commissaries: a mobile food truck and a commercial kitchen. One of the initial things food truck proprietors need to take care of is deciding which kind to choose. Just about every state or municipality requires food truck owners to operate out of a certified and licensed commercial commissary or kitchen. These facilities have to undergo approved inspection by health departments.

Basically, a commissary is a licensed commercial kitchen, food truck, or shared kitchen or food service facility. In some cases, cooking food is not allowed on the truck and is required to be cooked and prepared at the commissary. Normally, to satisfy state and municipal health departments, a commissary must have a three-sink compartment sink, one designated for dishwashing, one for dry and cold storage, and the kitchen must be licensed and inspected by the department of health and agriculture.

Chapter 5: Supplies and Equipment

If you are a cook, especially those who have earned some level of bragging rights, then you can fully understand the feeling of starting a meal prep, and you're missing some vital ingredient. This works the same way as a business owner.

Having everything at your disposal helps to achieve your goals when serving customers and giving them the best that you have to offer. They are all of the parts of the puzzle. For instance, beginning the right way determines how things will turn out in the end.

Cooking Equipment

When you're buying equipment for your food truck, you can expect to devote the bulk of your budget to cooking equipment. To optimize your food truck kitchen, you can select a mixture of countertop and full-size models. Devote more space to your most-used equipment and stick with countertop alternatives for appliances you will use less often or for smaller quantities of food.

A list of essential food truck cooking equipment is itemized here.

Griddle or Flat Top Grill: Griddles and grills are best for preparing dishes like pancakes, burgers, eggs, and vegetables.

Range: Ranges are useful for frying, sautéing, boiling, and simmering any food item like proteins and sauces.

Charbroiler: Charbroilers can assist you with making grilling marks and unique flavors on chicken, steaks, vegetables, and more.

Microwave: With microwaves, you can heat dishes and steam vegetables or seafood items.

Toaster: A toaster allows you to obtain perfect textured bread on sandwiches, breakfast items, bagels, waffles, and muffins.

Salamander or Cheese Melter: Salamanders are perfect for creating a browning effect on sandwiches or macaroni and cheese. This item is also good for melting cheese on casseroles.

Fryer: A fryer is essential for preparing popular food truck items like French fries, chicken tenders, and onion rings.

Warming and Holding Equipment

Warming and holding equipment is necessary in order to maintain menu items at safe temperatures.

This equipment helps to ward against contamination, illnesses, and health inspection violations. These are suggestions for warming and heating up food:

Countertop Food Warmer: This is a countertop warmer intended to maintain foods like pasta, vegetables, and casseroles at safe temperatures.

Fry Dump Station: A fry dump station helps warms fries when they are taken out of the fryer.

Soup Warmer or Kettle: Soup kettles help keep soups hot until being served.

food Prep Equipment

This food prep equipment is good for preparing and serving food will come in handy often. This should get you going in the beginning.

Stainless Steel Worktable: Stable steel worktables are used to provide additional food preparation workspace.

Cutting Boards: Cutting boards are convenient for dicing, chopping, and slicing.

Knives and Knife Rack: Choose good quality knives that can save you money in replacement costs in the long run. These work well when in compact kitchens.

Skillets or Frying Pans: Are often used for frying, sautéing, or steaming certain menu selections.

Saucepans: Saucepans can help reduce time in simmering or boiling sauces or broths. you to reduce, simmer, and boil sauces and broths.

Turners: Turners are essential items most often used for burgers and vegetables.

Thermometers: Thermometers help to keep food items safe when they are thoroughly cooked.

Blender or Food Processor: This equipment is best used for making smoothies, salsa, sauces, and soups along with a blender or food processor.

French Fry Cutter: If your food truck has fries on the menu, a French fry cutter is an essential item.

Serving Equipment and Disposables

Food trucks typically dispense on-the-go clientele which means you will have to stock up on disposable supplies. Prepare room in your truck for these items to make readily available and running out of them may mean closing shop for the day.

You can begin with these serving supplies:

Serving Utensils: Spoons, ladles, or tongs should be clean and on hand.

Pump Condiment Dispenser: Provide pump condiment dispensers outside your truck or self-serving customers. Make sure they are full at all times.

Squeeze Bottles. These bottles allow your customers the freedom to add condiments to their food on their own.

Sugar, Spice, and Cheese Shakers: Dust your offerings with any needed toppings with sugar, spices, and cheese.

Paper Food Trays: For serving your food truck's main or side dishes, food trays come in handy, especially during rush hours.

Paper, Foam, or Plastic Dinnerware: Disposable dinnerware works well if you serve large portions or plates.

Paper or Plastic Cups: Paper or plastic cups are necessary when serving beverages that don't come in a can or bottle.

Plastic Utensils: Disposable plastic utensils allow guests to help themselves and is vital to every food truck operation.

Take-Out Containers: Take-out containers allow on the go customers the ability to transport their food more easily.

Portion Cups: Portion cups help customers dispense the correct portion of condiments for their food items.

Paper Napkins and Dispenser: Be sure to place napkin dispensers in a convenient location outside of your truck.

Guest Checks or Order Forms: Guest checks and order forms are necessary in order to stay organized while preparing orders.

Disposable Gloves: Disposable gloves help you stay sanitary while serving and preparing food.

Aluminum or Plastic Food Wrap: These wraps come in handy when serving or storing food for later use.

Refrigeration Equipment

Refrigeration equipment keeps food and ingredients fresh. You can have a main refrigerator for main food items and another for sauces and toppings.

Consider this specialized refrigeration equipment.

Worktop or Undercounter Refrigerator: Worktop refrigerators serves dual roles as a workspace and compact space.

Sandwich or Salad Preparation Refrigerator: Sandwich or salad prep refrigerators are made with the bottom portion for chilled items and a top area for space to store pans, toppings, or preparation space.

Pizza Preparation Refrigerator: Pizza prep refrigerators serve as preparation models for sandwiches and provides a larger area to prepare pizzas.

Countertop Glass Door Refrigerator: A countertop glass door refrigerator offers solutions for the use of canned or bottled beverages on your food truck.

Janitorial Equipment

Janitorial equipment is vital for maintaining the cleanliness of your truck. These supplies are necessary and used daily.

Stock up your truck with these janitorial items.

Three-Compartment Sink: A three-compartment sink is required for operating food trucks. If you have the room, these sinks are useful for washing, rinsing, and sanitizing your dishes and dishware.

Hand Sink: This sink is used primarily to encourage employees to maintain good hygiene to keep food sanitary.

Anti-Fatigue or Wet Area Floor Mats: These mats are added protections from slip and fall while providing a cushion where you stand.

Sanitizing Chemicals: Sanitizing chemicals are intended for use on both surfaces and dishware.

Scrubbers and Sponges: Scrubbers and sponges are used to keep cooking utensils and dinnerware clean.

Trash Can and Liners: Keep the disposal area clean and tidy with ample trash can liners.

Broom and Dustpan: A broom and dustpan are great for housecleaning or tidying up the work area by cleaning spills and keeping the food truck floors clean.

Chapter 6: Sourcing Ingredients

Creating a firm foundation is key to your success in the food service business. It would serve a newcomer well to explore strategies and best practices many experts employ.

Sourcing, as referenced in the food business, is a process by purchasing goods and ingredients. Much like a food truck, the business or establishment sets the quantity or amount needed and makes purchases accordingly.

This process takes pre-planning on your part, meaning taking advance orders from customers and shopping with these necessities. When cooking, always remember to think ahead. Know how much fresh product you can store before it goes bad if you are ordering from a wholesaler. It is better to run short on food than to have an abundance of food items that is spoiled and has gone bad.

For novices, figuring out the exact quantity you'll need is usually a matter of trial and error. Places to source your food relies on advance planning on purchases and a determined schedule of offerings. Six sources to consider are:

1. Wholesaler food distributors. You can locate plenty of choices of food over the internet, from sites like Food Service.com or Business.com, which carry directories of food and drink suppliers. You can also try searching for food wholesalers directly in your area like Sysco, Performance Food Group, or US FoodService.

2. Manufacturers. There are several food manufacturers that are reachable and can sell to you or steer you in the right direction to locate products nearby. Start searching websites initially. Thousands of companies are available to consider. Small and niche companies are sometimes able to supply your product needs like apples or zucchini. There's someone out there who is ready to serve your company's needs. As with all things, be sure to compare prices along the way while looking at the quality of your mobile enterprise.

3. Local and regional suppliers. There are also food distributors available to you locally in your area. Such regional suppliers like Cheney Brothers or Smart and Final can be of assistance in the areas of distribution.

4. Greenmarkets and farmer's markets. Food trucks and food cart entrepreneurs should consider selling healthier organic versions of the popular food items in locating organic farms and greenmarkets. You may have to charge a little more to customers but you're then able to market to the health-conscious crowd which is a large demographic for some areas. Get acquainted with local growers and take the time to scout for the things you may need.

5. Food cooperative. Restaurateurs or mobile food owners can purchase food items collectively in bulk amounts to save money. The larger the quantity, the larger the discounts in many cases. Find noncompeting business owners and try to team up and form cooperatives. What this entails is a group of people who come together with a common goal for mutual benefits. Look in your very own neighborhoods for other interested parties who are interested in establishing a co-op. The Co-op Directory is a great resource for information.

6. Shopping clubs. Shopping clubs like BJ's Wholesale Club, Sam's Club, Costco, and others are becoming very popular these days for shopping for quality goods in bulk. Many food

truck owner patronize these shopping clubs. An annual membership commitment is usually required to get in on these reasonably priced items.

Chapter 7: Developing the Menu

Consider food trends.

One area you should research is food trends when deciding on your niche and menu for your business. Your food truck might be based on a fad, which isn't a long term ideal. The food trends to research are things like gluten-free, no GMO, organic, and vegetarian options.

Are there other food trucks in your area with your theme? If so, how will you be different?

The Food Network and gourmet magazines like Gourmet and Bon Appetite are valuable resources. It is their job to report on and cover design and food trends. They know what's going on in the industry.

Watch celebrity chefs!

Your concept should be something fun that you will love doing every single day of your life, never regret the decision - baby it, grow it, and make money at it.

One thing you don't want to get stuck in is a fad. For instance, frozen yogurt was a fad, and now those shops are gone. Tacos, even from a food truck, are established fare. They are evolving into fish tacos and other flavors.

You might just want to bring your ethnic food to the city or to your own community. There are many Little Vietnam, Little Havana, China Towns in major cities. These areas support independent food ventures.

Stay true to yourself.

Do not stop until you have the perfect idea that reflects you, implement market research, and be precise in your theme.

You won't get the funding you need if you are just blowing in the wind.

No matter what the food is that you serve, it must be different from what diners would find in other eating establishments - distinctive, attractive, and exciting. Locally sourced food is a growing trend with prix fixe menu items that change frequently.

Pricing and Profit

A major way of ensuring profit is by having a great menu. You must balance food cost, the price charged, and have a range of inexpensive and expensive items.

Food cost is about 30%-35%. So, for every $1.00 you pay for a food item, you need to charge a minimum of $3.34. The rule of thumb is to calculate the cost of your dish and mark up about 3 times that cost.

Food cost is the menu price. Cost of food is how much you paid for the ingredients.

Food costs are made up of ingredients and everything else in your food truck from payroll, to rent or mortgage payment. The food is bought and paid for. Someone must prepare it. It must be cooked, served, and cleaned up afterward.

The formula is:

- Cost of your product /.35

Let's look at the example of a steak dinner:

- Steak = $5.00/portion, your cost

- Wrap = $2.50/plate (Potato or vegetable, salad, bread, and condiments)

- $7.50/.35 = $21.43

$21.43 is the absolute minimum. However, it is an awkward number. You could put $21.50 or $21.99 on your menu. This brings your food cost just at 30%, bringing in more profit.

Consider the example of a fabulous burger with lettuce, tomato, onion, and fries — the cost to you $3.00. Your cost-plus profit is now $8.57.

Offer other up-sell options and more favored choices. Maybe even offer a signature burger with various cheese, mushrooms, avocado, etc. The cost goes up to $3.30. Your food cost is now $9.43.

While you are pricing your cost of food, you must further determine if a specific item truly belongs on your menu.

For instance, your overhead cost, cost of food, and drink plus tax comes to $15.00 for a lunch dish. Let's say that your customer only wants to pay $10.00-$11.00 for that same lunch. This lunch item should come off your menu.

On the other hand, some items on your menu are loss leaders, much like a retail store. Something is sold at cost or slightly above because your specific target market will add appetizers, drinks, and dessert to their total bill.

Portion Control

This brings up portion control. You are giving away your profits if you put too much food on a plate. Conversely, you are losing customers if there is less food than expected. Customers then feel this is a great deal or a bad value, respectively.

Your business will reflect the results immediately. You will either be eating into your profits or losing customers.

Every dish must be the exact same every time: same weight, same look. Practicing portion control begins with measuring every item.

Meat and seafood must be measured. Cheese and some other condiments can be stored already in pre-portioned packages. Others can be measured with a measuring cup like vegetables and mashed potatoes, for instance.

Eventually, you can eyeball portions. However, double-check your 'eyeball' amount every so often. It has a way of getting away from you.

Let's say you're offering a 4-oz steak entrée with a baked potato side. The steak must be exactly 4 oz. and the baked potato must be the exact weight you have determined, every single time.

You could offer an option between a 4-oz. and a 6-oz. steak or you can offer a ¼ lb. or ½ pound hamburger.

Steaks, fish, shrimp, and chicken breasts can be purchased already packaged in individual portion-sized packages.

The same rule applies to sandwiches and salads. For sandwiches, count out the number of meat and cheese slices, possibly including a different price point for certain variations of bread.

Add up condiments and each topping, such as lettuce and tomato.

Pricing Tips and Tricks

Keep track of the wholesale price of food items. Seasonal changes, weather, and gas prices can change at any time. Adjust your cost of food, i.e., menu prices, accordingly.

The way to do this goes back to balancing your menu between expensive and less expensive items. Expensive items are more susceptible to price variables, while less expensive items are more likely to remain steady.

Don't get into the time and expense of changing your menu every few weeks. If you use a chalkboard, whiteboard, or your own printed menu, changes are easier to make.

Understand your cost of food, price fluctuations, portion control, maintaining a balanced menu, and customer expectations. These are changes you can count on when crunching numbers and determining profits and revenue.

Before moving on to the creative aspect of designing your menu, let's outline a few additional things to study, research, and be aware of concerning your menu.

•   Some food truck owners price their items on a gross margin basis. Determine what you should make per item and add that to your cost of food.

• According to Cornell University and the National Food Truck Association, 60% of food trucks fail within the first three years of opening, and after five years, the number may climb as high as 75%.

• The more successful food trucks average a net profit at or over 30% of sales. With consistent returns like this, you could pay your investment off in at least three years. That's an awesome ROI.

• Food trucks can fail because they don't have a unique selling point. Why should your customers come to your food truck versus your competitors'?

• Great food and service are not a unique selling point. Everyone is advertising the same thing. This goes back to your concept, theme, passion, and emotion. The WHY you are in the food industry business.

• Can you negotiate prices? You need to know what other food trucks are paying for food items and make your suppliers compete for your business. You know the saying, 'there's a sucker in every negotiation.' Don't let it be you.

A large menu is confusing to customers and lacks focus. Large menus require more ordering time, a larger inventory of food, longer ticket times, equipment, and cooks. The longer this takes, the less amount of time you are making profits.

Creative Production

Your menu development and design are not random decisions. They are a significant part of your food truck concept. Your menu defines you.

Menus will vary by the concept. Some will be busy with a lot of information crammed into every nook and cranny.

Some will be big, and plastic coated, maybe written on a chalk or whiteboard.

Menus have everything to do with the impact you make on your customers, carrying out your theme, and giving focus to your food.

A cost-effective, profitable menu is of small or moderate size, as in the number of dishes offered.

The main message is the dishes you're known for, the food that separates you from the rest, and deals that can be supplemented by seasonal and short-term offers.

You have your theme and concept in place. You know your target market and the food you are going to serve, so now it is time to make everything work together. What holds it together is the core menu.

However you implement your menu. It speaks volumes about you, your food truck, and your food.

Chapter 8: Running the Business

Let's talk about how to run your new food truck from top to bottom. In this chapter, we'll discuss formulating a business plan, what a day in the life of a food truck owner looks like, some accounting tips and advice, and how to hire and manage employees.

Business Plan

 A business plan is two things:

📍 A roadmap for the success of your food truck focused on reaching your financial and personal goals.

📍 A road map leading to obtaining financing and persuading others to invest in your dream.

Writing a business plan sounds like a daunting task, but it shouldn't be.

Just be clear and concise.

Keep it short.

No one is going to read hundreds of pages that you have slaved over. Start with a cover page, followed by a Table of Contents, then go on from there.

Business plans will vary by the type of food truck you are planning.

Using any free information from the internet does not necessarily preclude you from soliciting a professional. Perhaps you do the hard work and have a professional review it to give you input and advice. Your banker or other investors may help as well.

Gabri's Food Truck is a fine-dining food truck. We focus on our new American-Swedish menu with a touch of Asian influence. We will be located in the booming, and rapidly expanding, a borough of Long Branch, New Jersey 'on the shore.'

The outlook for the future of Long Branch is promising. Developers are recreating a $150 million first-class resort project. The old pier will be rebuilt with ferry service to Manhattan, New York City, beach cabanas, with a boardwalk and a bike path over a total of 25 acres. There will be 100,000 sq. ft. of commercial space, and over 700 residential units with condo and townhouses ranging from $200,000-$500,000; rentals from $1000-$2,500 a month, and a two-tier parking garage. The combination of these elements will provide the city with a year-round economy.

The menu will be inspired by different countries' specialties and appeal to a diverse clientele. You can get Swedish specialties like herring, gravlax, and meatballs, or you can go a little bit more International and choose a red curry chicken with basmati rice, or an Asian grilled shrimp with spinach, tofu, and black bean sauce. The menu will change every 3-4 months but keep the favorites. Prices will be competitive with other upscale food trucks in the area.

The food truck will be open seven days a week. We will offer special theme nights to attract new customers to Gabri's. The food truck will be fine dining. During the busy summer months, we will offer a special summer menu featuring lighter fare, exotic drinks, as well as non-alcoholic offerings.

The service will be relaxed, very friendly, and accurate. We will hire the best people available, training, motivating, and encouraging them, and thereby retaining the friendliest, most efficient, staff possible. Our management team is comprised of individuals whose backgrounds consist of 50 years' experience in foodservice, food truck, hotel, catering, management, finance, marketing, art, and motion pictures.

Catering will be a major part of the business. "Leave it to Linda Catering" already has an established clientele, and we are growing each and every day. We feel with today's hectic work schedules, customers don't always have time to set up that birthday party or any other special event. Now customers can leave it to the pros and receive the finest, most memorable party or special occasion, ever. We have years of experience in the catering business and know what an important client wants and needs. We will have a large International menu for customers to select from, and we will offer full catering services providing everything from table settings to the dessert. We anticipate our total sales allocation to be 85% of food truck sales and 15% from catering sales. The combined cost of sales will be 33%, producing a gross profit of 67% on total sales.

The most important factor to us is our financial success, and we believe this will be achieved by offering high-quality service and excellent food with an interesting twist. We have created financial projections based on our experience and knowledge of the area. With a start-up expenditure of $385,000, we can generate $1,085,465 in sales by the end of year two, and produce good net profits by the end of year three.

We are seeking an SBA 7(A) loan guaranty for $200,000 with a 7% interest rate. We are investing $60,000 of our own capital and seeking to raise an additional $125,000 from investors. Our preferred instrument will be five-year subordinated notes with an attractive coupon rate of 12% for the first two years and 15% for the remaining three years. At the end of five years, the investors' notes will have matured, and the original principal plus a 2% premium, and the final interest payment will be made. Our investment philosophy is conservative.

Since food truck start-ups are so speculative, our belief and commitment to our investors will be to pay a generous, predictable rate of return, while not strangling our operational cash flow. As our business becomes more established and reliable, our ability to pay an improved return of capital will be evidenced by an increased coupon rate of 15% of the original principal. At maturity, we feel it proper to retire the notes with a 2% premium to the original principal invested.

following the Executive Summary

Gabri's Executive Summary is a bit hard to read. Overall, you want to tell a story. Your readers and potential investors want to hear your story, but write it in an easy to read format.

Shorter paragraphs, for instance, and with fewer passive sentences. Also, spell-check and proofread your summary. The Gabri's summary is being quoted here, word for word.

The rest of your business plan includes various parts of the following. The final amount of material you write should be governed by the size and type of your food truck.

1.0 Executive Summary (example above)	1.1 Mission	1.2 Objectives	1.3 Keys to Success
2.0 Company Summary	2.1 Company Ownership	2.2 Start-up Summary	3.0 Services
3.1 Pricing and Profitability	4.0 Market Analysis	4.1 Market Segmentation	4.2 Target Market Segment

	Summary		Strategy
5.0 Strategy and Implementation Summary	5.1 Competitive Edge	5.1.1 Main Competitors	5.2 Marketing Strategy
5.2.1 Marketing Program	5.3 Sales Strategy	5.3.1 Sales Forecast	5.4 Milestones
6.0 Web Plan Summary	7.0 Management Summary	7.1 Management Team	7.2 Personnel Plan
8.0 Financial Plan	8.1 Important Assumptions	8.2 Break-even Analysis	8.3 Projected Profit and Loss
8.4 Projected Cash Flow	8.5 Projected Balance Sheet	8.6 Business Ratios	8.7 Exit Strategy
9.0 Sample Menus	10.0 Appendix		

Daily life

You'll work the most (and longest) hours. You'll work every job in the business, from line cook to mechanic to accountant. To create a successful food truck business, you'll need to develop a culture of hard work, with you being the one setting the example for your staff.

Sure, it can be a 9-to-5 job, but not in the way you may expect. Take a look into a day in the life of a food truck owner. (Keep in mind that your schedule will look different if you opt for a different service time, such as breakfast or lunch.)

9 a.m. to noon

The alarm goes off, and you crawl out of bed; it's 9 a.m. From the time you wake up until approximately two hours later, you're busy going over your calendar of events and planning for your day. With 30 minutes to go before meeting with your team members, it's time to get ready and drive to your meet-up location, the commercial kitchen.

Noon to 12:30 p.m.

You meet with your team to discuss your notes, daily specials, and suggestions from lessons learned the previous day. Your team shares with you what they've heard overnight from local news and from customers and competitors. Sharing this information keeps everyone in the loop, part of the team, and, in most cases, in high spirits.

12:30 p.m. to 5:30 p.m.

During this time, the team goes to the market and bakery or to inventory the food shipments that have been delivered. After getting the food needed for the truck, everyone heads to the commercial kitchen to chop fruits and vegetables, blend the sauces, and grill the meat (if you serve it).

Those team members not involved in the food prep will organize the truck to ready it for the work night, fire up their Twitter and Facebook accounts to notify followers of the truck's location(s), and conduct another round of correspondence and phone calls.

5:30 p.m. to 6 p.m.

Time to head to your "office." You now take the truck from the commercial kitchen's lot to your first stop.

6 p.m. to 2:30 a.m.

It's time! It's time to open the doors, practice your trade, and make your mark on your community. When you reach your destination and a line of people are already at the curb, the sight is both invigorating and terrifying.

It's invigorating because you already have loyal followers who have found your location and are waiting to be served a meal from your heart. It's terrifying because you need to park and start cooking quickly, so you aren't keeping your customers waiting too long.

Now is when you must enjoy your job; now is the point where you'll know whether you've made the proper choice in opening a food truck. If you're distracted or dislike your environment, you may want to start planning how to sell your investment and head to another career.

2:30 a.m. to 5 a.m.

The night's service is over, and you've made your way back to the commercial kitchen. You clean out the truck and wash it down, so it's ready for the next shift. You break down and marinate the meat and, in some cases, even order the bread for tomorrow's pick-up or delivery.

You store the food and lock up the truck. It's finally time to head home.

On the trip home, you reflect back on the day and are very thankful that the oil in the fryer didn't explode or that you were able to start the truck without any issues, and finally, you see it — home sweet home. After a final round of reading e-mails and listening to phone messages, you go to bed. Your 9-to-5 workday is over, only to start again tomorrow.

1. Open a business bank account. You must keep your personal finances separate from your business finances.

2. Hire help. This is why people get accounting and finance degrees because it sometimes takes more knowledge than one generally possesses.

3. Track your expenses. Everything needs a receipt.

4. Establish procedures. Having a system, being organized, and completing tasks on a daily, weekly, monthly, quarterly, and yearly schedule is important.

5. Know what's going on. Even if you hire an accountant or bookkeeper, be in the know about what's going with your numbers.

Hiring and Managing Staff

Let's discuss how to find and hire the right people.

I broke this staffing section into a multi-step process, and I will discuss each in detail.

1. Where to find the right people to hire.

The best practices for hiring qualified staff are through using advertising in a way that covers your city and not just in your direct neighborhood.

I have three suggestions on where to advertise:

A.   Run an ad on Craigslist. You may be surprised how often people look for jobs on Craigslist. Craigslist is an essential tool for a lot of things, from selling your old couch and bicycle to hiring people to do your yard or other small projects, to hiring new employees. I use Craigslist every time I need help. I even hired a great bookkeeper from there.

B.   Word of mouth. You can ask some of your other employees if they know of anyone they can recommend. Ask your friends or other business owners that you know well. This way, you at least have a reference.

C.   Hiring employees from other local businesses. This practice sounds bad, I know, but you are not doing anything illegal or unethical. Let me explain in an example.

You go to your local burger joint, and the lady that took your order was very courteous and professional. Strike up a conversation with her, compliment her on her professionalism, let her know you own a food truck, and you are looking to hire some good employees.

Ask her if she knows anyone that she can recommend. Give her your business card. You will see that out of five people you meet this way, three will call you either with a recommendation, or they will call to apply for themselves.

There are three reasons she may contact you to apply for a job for herself:

•   Obviously, people love compliments.

•   Most employees do not feel appreciated enough at their current jobs.

•   Everyone wants to move up at their job and eventually make more money.

2. Creating a good application.

Now that you have some applicants calling you, you need to give them each an application, right? Where do you get these job applications?

I am sure you can go to the local office supply store and pick up a stack of them but is that a good idea? Those applications are very generic and not designed for your type of business.

When preparing a job application, there are a few things to keep in mind:

•   Make absolutely no mention of their social security number on the application.

•   It is also a good idea not to ask about race on a job application

•   Make sure to ask about their education level

•   Ask about their previous employment history

•   Ask how many addresses they have lived at in the last five years.

These last three aspects can tell you much about a person.

If an applicant held one job for the last 5 years, lived in one address in that 5 years and has a high school education, chances are that they will be a good employee, compared to if an applicant had 4 jobs in the last 5 years, moved 3 times in that same period, and does not have a high school diploma.

When asking about previous employment, make sure to ask the name and contact information of the company along with the name of their supervisors. This way, you can check their references.

It is a common practice for employers not to reveal any details of a current or former employee, so if you ask whether they were good or bad at their job, you may not get a straight answer.

Previous employers can tell you if the applicant can be rehired. Your answer lies in that if they say the applicant can be rehired, you know they are saying they do recommend that person.

3. Asking the right questions during the interview.

Once you find some good applicants, call a few of them for an interview.

A few of the factors I test for when interviewing:

•   I always give them a simple math test to see if they can calculate basic addition and subtraction in their head.

•   Ask a few hypothetical questions ranging from how to handle a customer service issue to an emergency situation. For example, "If someone ought to get sick, what would you do and how would you handle that emergency?"

•   Ask them if they have any physical limitations which may prevent them from performing the normal duties and responsibilities of a food truck job.

Next, I usually ask if they can obtain a background check from the local police dept. I offer to pay for that cost. It saves money and time to have them provide you with that report instead of you running a background check on them.

Before you hire a new employee, make it clear that it is your company policy to hire people with a 60 days probation period. Meaning, they can be let go within these 60 days without giving them any reasons, based on their performance.

Once you hire them, there is some basic paperwork that you need to have them fill out. Some new hire paperwork includes:

A.   A completed job application that you already have

B.   W-4 form from the IRS, which indicates the employee's desired tax withholdings.

C.   New hire handbook. You should create this document based on your own rules, regulations, and best practices.

D.   A signed disclaimer about the 60-day probation period, which would explain, in writing, that for the next 60 days, they are on probation and their employment can be terminated for any reason.

E.   A copy of their criminal background check.

F.   A copy of their social security card and Driver's license.

Some states require you to register all new employees you hire with the DOL(Department of Labor) within seven days of hiring them. If this step is neglected, there will be a fine imposed on you. Check with your state's DOL and see if they require it.

Find out if your state is an "employment-at-will state." This means that you can terminate anyone at any time without giving them a reason. This practice sounds odd, I know, and maybe I am oversimplifying it.

The essence is that you really do not have to give them much of a reason for the termination.

4. Providing proper training.

Once you hire an employee, it is important to provide them with proper training.

First, give them a tour of the food truck. Show them how the whole process of your food truck works. Explain their job duties and responsibilities, like what is expected of them before they start and after they end their shifts.

I usually provide three full days of training before I let any new employees work a shift all by themselves.

The appearance of your employees is the most important first impression on your customer; you do not get a second chance to create that first impression. Make sure your employees are in uniform.

Your team needs to know your marketing strategy so they can effectively promote your food truck.

Let me explain.

Even though most food trucks show their specials right on top of the menu or on a display board, I strongly believe mentioning the special by name and explaining how and why it is such a great special makes customers more inclined to opt-in.

The power of face-to-face marketing can be a very powerful thing.

5. Motivating and empowering your employees.

You need to make sure your employees do not feel that this is a dead-end job. To do so, you need to motivate them.

Typically there are three ways that you can motivate your employees:

1.	Tell them how to earn raises. I typically tell all new hires that I would start them at a certain hourly rate, then after 60 days, they will get a raise to a slightly higher hourly rate. Every 6 months, I will do a performance review. If they are performing well, they can earn a raise.

2.   Another great way to motivate your staff is just simply by telling them they are doing a great job, give them compliments when you see good work, acknowledge them, and show them you noticed. A simple "thank you," and a pat on the back can go a long way sometimes. Remember, everybody wants to feel appreciated.

If you see an employee did a great job handling a bad situation, or they showed some exceptional quality or ability which is beyond their daily work duties and responsibilities, reward them by acknowledging their efforts.

Perhaps you can buy them lunch or have lunch with them as a special thanks. It can mean a lot to them. Give them a gift certificate for a movie or a pizza. This can make them feel appreciated and proud to be a part of your team. Often, I will set up certain goals and offer incentives if my employees reach the goal.

You can be very creative when it comes to creating an incentive program, but it depends on what type of food truck you have. Reaching a specific goal (selling a certain number of desserts, having a lunch rush sales goal, etc.) can be very motivating. Perhaps you could even make it a friendly competition and offer cash or other incentives.

6. How to discipline bad behavior.

Let's face the truth that we don't always hire the best employees. There are bad apples in every bunch, right? How do you discipline bad behavior when you see it?

It could be that someone is not doing their job properly or giving poor customer service, not doing their side work, or even showing up for work late more than once in the same week. It might be nothing too serious.

If you witness truly bad behavior, a direct violation of your company policy, or insubordination - where you asked them to perform a duty, and they refuse - these are grounds for immediate termination, and no other disciplinary action is needed.

For minor issues, as I mentioned earlier, you can give them a verbal warning first and monitor them to see if there is any improvement. If not, you can then give them a written warning.

Most companies nowadays have formal written warning forms where you can indicate the action that they took, which was not proper or the job that they did not perform even after a prior verbal warning.

Have all parties involved sign the form. Keep a copy of it in their employment file. I usually terminate an employee if he or she makes the same violation within 30 days of giving them the written warning.

7. Hold regular employee meetings and coaching.

Last but not least, it is very important to have regularly scheduled employee meetings and coaching. Meet at least once a month.

In this meeting, inform your employees of any upcoming changes, ask for any issues they faced that month, any concerns they have, and implement new incentive plans you have for them for the following month.

Offer them tips and words of encouragement. Remind them to greet and make eye contact with each customer. Also, emphasize the cleaning regiment and the importance of keeping their assigned areas clean.

Chapter 9: Growing the Business

Social media is a must. Don't even think of not using it!

82% of business from millennials comes through social media. This is where the action is, and the game is played.

Michael Lukianoff, Fishbowl's Chief Analytics Officer, told CNBC in an interview that "social media gives smaller, independent, and regional [brands] a level playing ground to get their message/voice out."

The industry is telling you that you are not competing successfully with other food trucks if you are not on social media. As the competition heats up, the stronger your presence on social media should be.

##

Let's talk about the BIG social media for food trucks called Yelp.

1.   Get your free page on Yelp as soon as possible. Log on to their website, sign up, add photos, and create a Yelp Deal. Yelp provides the ability to add deals, photos, and messaging. According to Yelp, listings with photos keep visitors on that page 2½ times longer than those without. https://www.yelp.com/

2.   Yelp and Bing are joining forces. Yelp information is now integrated into Bing Local Pages. Searchers are now able to scan your food truck, location, and reviews directly from their Bing results. https://www.bing.com/

3.   Yelp releases mobile data often. Previously they reported:

a.   Yelpers called a local business every other second via the mobile application.

b.   35 percent of all searches on Yelp.com came from a Yelp mobile app.

c.   Every other second, a consumer had generated directions to a local business.

d.   A photo was uploaded every 30 seconds from a Yelp mobile app.

You can purchase reports from Yelp at around $3.00 to keep up with trends and identify innovative ideas for your food truck.

The Big 6

The key social media outlets are Facebook, Twitter, Pinterest, LinkedIn, YouTube, and Instagram.

•   Start your own blog. Blogging has been known to increase lead generation by 89%. Nurture these potential, loyal customers.

•   Find food bloggers and make them your friends. It's unbelievable how much promotion gets done through blogs. Even niche-marketing. Invite your food bloggers to share recipes, even host an event just for them.

- Tweet often.

- Post to Instagram and Facebook every day. Build ordering onto your Facebook page. You can indicate an 'Order Now' call to action button.

- Take tempting photos of your food with a good camera or use a professional. Make these your go-to social media posts.

- Offer coupons on Facebook and other social media. Include specials and holiday events, TGIFs, graduations, whatever fits with your style.

- Always respond to comments and complaints made by followers - good or bad. Positively resolve issues in the public forum. Use the opportunities to interact with customers with thanks directly, offer rewards, conduct contests, etc.

- Get on YouTube. Show off your food truck, have your chef or employees demonstrate a recipe. Show your location.

- Build a professional, functional, and attractive but fun website. You can hire companies to do this for you or create one of your own on a site like https://www.wix.com/.

- Capture information from each website visitor building a target market list.

- Capture customer phone numbers from call-ins, give discounts, vouchers, and coupons to customers who volunteer their information.

- With data that can be used for target marketing, use an email autoresponder technology to send gifts and awards for occasions, etc. A super good marketing email program is https://www.constantcontact.com/, but it's not free. You will have to pay for this service.

Traditional Marketing and PR

In addition to Yelp, social media, and your website landing page, you can choose various traditional advertising and marketing formats.

Traditional advertising and marketing include:

- Radio

- TV

- Print publications

- Billboards

These more traditional advertising methods can be expensive. Stretch your advertising dollars over the opportunities that provide a good ROI (Return on Investment).

Some examples of cheap public relations (PR) include:

- Writing a press release announcing something new

- Invite a local food editor to your food truck to submit a review to their column or publication

- Take out ads with offers in local papers, shoppers, and neighborhood magazines

- Sponsor a local sports team. Provide jerseys, if possible.

The most important rules of your core marketing program are:

1. Your target market must know you exist. This means being unique. This applies to the quality of food, service, friendliness, and cleanliness. Don't be unforgettable.

2.   You must get your customers to talk about you. Of course, the best advertising is word of mouth. Every customer that visits your food truck should feel as though they have had a real treat. If they don't have a pleasant experience, they won't be back. Anything they have to say will not be good.

3.   Messages you put out into the public must be clear, concise, and direct. Everyone gets hit with thousands of marketing and advertising messages every day.

4.   You and your business must be involved in the community. Be the single sponsor of a good community cause. Don't just show up or put your food truck's name on a t-shirt, but really get involved. People remember those that commit to helping them.

Marketing starts before you even open your food truck.

If you are not an expert, hire one, at least for the short term. You need to take advantage of all PR and marketing opportunities. It will be worth every single dime you spend to hire a professional who knows the food truck industry.

There are dozens of ways to promote your food truck. Identify those ways that make you stand out. Spend money on big ROI opportunities. Look for opportunities that are free or nearly free.

It doesn't matter how good you are at what you do, but without paying customers, your well-honed craft is just a hobby. Marketing is the way businesses attract and retain customers.

You may have survived thus far off word of mouth, but to build a long-lasting and profitable business, you'll likely need more than the occasional recommendation from friends and past customers. To grow and thrive, you'll need to market your business, which means sharing and spreading your brand, the services you offer and yourself, as an expert in your field.

But, before you can start marketing, you need to refine your brand image and determine how you'll apply it to your online, print, and social media presence.

This means figuring out the fonts, layouts, graphics, and information that best represent your business, and that will be most appealing to your target audience. Then put it all in writing. Reference it every time you roll out a new ad campaign or marketing initiative.

When it comes to brand building, consistency is key. Not only does consistency convey professionalism, but it also has a direct effect on your bottom line.

Consistency in written and visual communications makes it easier for costumers to understand the food you offer and your expertise in making that food. It lends legitimacy to your brand. And, over time, it builds trust. All of which adds to your ability to attract and retain customers.

To ensure consistency, create a brand guide that describes your company's mission, the menu you offer, the reason you do what you do, and how you will convey that message in the material you create.

It should also include your business' value proposition, aka your niche, or what it is about your food that attracts customers. Brand guides don't need to be exhaustive, but they should include notes on tone and style for written communications, as well as color palettes and styles for visual communications.

Your brand guide should cover:

• Brand Colors

- Logo Usage

- Logo Placement

- Iconography

- Fonts and Typography

- Graphic Styles

- Tone of Voice

- Signage Specs

You may also want to include:

- Editorial Guidelines

- Letterhead Design

- Business Card Design

- Image Filters

- Media Formatting

Including editorial guidelines and information on media, formatting may seem like a waste of time, but it will come in handy in the future when you add or update website pages, hire office help, or if you hire a third-party company to manage your website or social media accounts.

To ensure consistency, try to review all content and materials to ensure they meet your brand guidelines as they are generated. For many new image-conscious businesses, this comes easy at first.

However, over time, it's easy to let consistency reviews go by the wayside as business picks up or life outside work gets busy. When this happens, make a point to schedule brand consistency reviews on a monthly, bi-monthly, or quarterly basis.

Marketing Your New Business

You may have already started your marketing process without even realizing it. Marketing isn't limited to paid advertisements, trade show booths, or witty schemes that generate buzz.

Marketing starts off a lot smaller. Literally. Business cards are one of the first marketing endeavors many new businesses take, but they're one of the most important. Your website and online presence is also a form of marketing.

In this section, we'll review the different ways to market the food truck business and grow your customer base. We'll cover seven areas of marketing and offer some additional food for thought as you move on in the marketing process.

Areas of Marketing:

- Print Materials

- Digital Presence

- Social Media

- Paid Advertisements

- Networking

- Relationship Building

- Volunteering

Print Materials

As mentioned above, marketing starts with your business card. A well-designed, professionally printed, and concise business card establishes credibility and professionalism and helps people remember you.

If possible, order at least three boxes of business cards. Make it a practice of handing them out. Always carry them with you — you never know when you are going to meet a new customer or bump into the manager of a coveted venue — and don't risk running out — order new ones, well before you need them.

Informative brochures are a powerful marketing tool when meeting with prospective clients, working trade shows, and networking with industry peers. Since they are often handed out together, make sure your brochure matches the style and image embodied by your business card.

Like it or not, people will make snap judgments on you and your business based on the quality and design of your brochure. Clean, professional designs that highlight your menu and specialty are best.

However, keep your ideal client in mind when designing your brochure. Fancy card stock is great for high-budget clients, but if you're aiming for a budget-conscious crowd, consider a simpler look and feel.

Whenever possible, include a few professional quality photos of past events, customer testimonials, and a photo of yourself.

Your digital presence is an important marketing tool, and as a new business, it's one you need to stay on top of to gain an edge in competitive market places.

When a prospective client Googles "taco food trucks (your local area)," if your food truck isn't near the top of page one, you've probably already lost them. If you fail to rank on page one altogether, you definitely have.

Getting ranked at the top of page one isn't rocket science, however, the more local competition you have, the more challenging it becomes. One way to help your rank is to use your business name as your domain name.

It comes down to SEO, or search engine optimization, the algorithms for which, unfortunately, change over time.

If you can afford one, consider hiring a consultant, site designer, or manager who specializes in SEO. If doing so isn't in your budget, search for topical, free or low-cost classes or seminars.

Or, invest time in learning the basics of SEO reading about it online or with a free trial period on an online learning platform, like skillshare.

In addition to creating pages on social media sites, which we'll get to in the next section, you can increase your online presence through a blog.

Blogging is a simple, no-cost way to share your insights and expertise with a wide audience of potential clients. And, it has the potential to be a powerful marketing tool when wielded correctly.

There are a few things to keep in mind when it comes to blogging. Regularly updated blogs tend to be the most successful. You don't have to write a new one twice a week or even every week, but you should plan to update it at regular intervals, ideally no less than once a month.

Don't approach your blog as an advertisement for your business, instead think of it as a way to establish yourself as an expert in the field of food trucks.

Example topics may include a new vegan dinner recipe, the hottest trends in food trucks, details about an upcoming public event you're working on, or an inside look at the hottest new venue in town.

Regardless of the specific topic, always link blogs back to your website and make sure to feature your blog feed on your website.

Finally, when it comes to digital marketing, consider email marketing. Email marketing is a great way to keep your contacts up-to-date. Although you can bc your entire contact list without the assistance of special programming, employing email marketing software is recommended.

Programs like MailChimp, Constant Contact, GetResponse, and AWeber offer templates, email tracking, segmented lists, and a slew of interesting insights and automated features for an easier, faster, and more fruitful experience.

Social Media

You should make business pages on as many platforms as are popular in your area. But, avoid thinking of them as advertisements. Also, avoid thinking of them as your accounts.

Your business pages should be managed separately from your personal pages. Ensure your approval is required before posts from others appear on your wall or feed. And never post anything personal on a business page.

Your Facebook business page should include information on your services, your contact info, links to your website and blog, and images of past events.

Use Twitter to tweet out quick tidbits about events you're planning, like a map to parking for an upcoming event.

Create a professional page on LinkedIn and use it to showcase your business and expertise, meet new clients, and network with fellow industry professionals.

There are many interesting and fun marketing campaigns designed specifically for social media. Remember the ice bucket challenge? It was viral marketing at its best — all aimed at raising awareness of ALS.

A less note-worthy, but often used social media marketing strategy is the share and save. This simple strategy only requires you create a post with your logo on it, let people know that if they share it (number of choice) times, they'll receive a (number of choice) discount, then track the shares.

Once you start paying attention, you'll start seeing social media marketing campaigns every time you log on, and before long, you'll be coming up with your own creative and fun social media marketing campaigns.

Although not generally thought of as social media sites, review sites like Yelp, Google Local, and Yahoo Local are increasingly popular places for customers to share their experiences with others.

Consider listing your business on one or more of these review sites. Opt to be notified of new reviews, whenever it is an option, and make a point of personally responding to all reviews, especially is they lean negative.

Paid Advertisements

Depending on the area you live in and the clients you're marketing to, you may want to consider paid advertisements local radio or TV stations, or in local or regional magazines or newspapers.

While advertising can get pretty costly, it doesn't start out that way. One form of paid advertisement, that's generally pretty cheap, and surprisingly still affective, is listing your number in the Yellow Pages.

In print, advertising costs increase with the size and color quality of the ad. While a one-inch black and white ad in the classified business section of your local paper won't cost you much, chances are it won't yield much business either.

If you're going to pay for an advertisement, choose the location wisely.

Or, skip the newspapers and magazines altogether and opt for direct mail. But before you do this, you'll need to make sure you have a finely curated mailing list of potential clients likely to respond to paper mail. Such lists can be purchased online from a list broker. A word of caution, before you buy, research the best broker services for your target market and read customer reviews of each contender.

Networking

Networking is an essential part of marketing, especially for business owners. But if the header on this section made you grimace, don't skip this section just yet.

Networking isn't schmoozing with strangers or taking every opportunity possible, even when unwarranted, to bring up your business. Good networking, successful networking, is much more subtle than that.

Networking can be a learning experience that enables you to provide better service to your clients. Start attending local functions. These types of events can be great for collecting ideas.

Bring your business cards and freely offer one up when you make a connection with a potential client or someone you may want to work with in the future, but don't feel pressured to sell your services. You're there to get inspired. Think of the networking that will likely naturally occur as an added perk.

Another way to network is to join local business groups and associations, where you can meet local professionals who you may want to call upon for service down the road.

You don't have to sell yourself, but you should be open to forming working relationships with business professionals.

When it comes down to it, networking is all about meeting new people and building relationships.

Relationship Building

When you meet someone in the industry who you'd like to work with in the future, make an effort to build a relationship with them.

Add them to your holiday card list or shoot them an email a couple of times a year to congratulate them on a specific event or award, or to wish them a happy birthday.

In general, relationship building is about letting them know you remember and appreciate them. Relationship building with potential customers is more of a process. It's important to spend time talking to them, really listening, and making sure they feel heard. And, never make them feel rushed.

Volunteer

Giving back is a great way to get something back and feel good while doing it. If you're looking to get your name out there and grow your business, consider volunteering.

Consider offering your services to a local community group that holds multiple events/fundraisers a year. Local Boosters clubs are a great example. They raise funds for the teams and clubs at the local high school through raffles, events, and other fundraisers throughout the year. Find out where they meet or who is in charge, then offer your services catering or providing food for an event for them.

With all they do, these groups are usually rather receptive to professional help. By lending a hand, you'll not only be getting your name out there with club members, but you'll be showcasing your skills for everyone who attends the event.

And, oftentimes, professionals who volunteer their time are given special thanks in programs or pamphlets passed out at the door.

Volunteering is a great way to get your name out there and grow brand recognition, but before you start offering your services all around town, there are a few things to keep in mind.

Determine the value you'll receive from volunteering your services for a particular event.

In addition to the type of event, consider who the guests are and how many there will be to determine the amount of exposure to ideal clients each event offers.

Never give more time than you can afford to give. Volunteering feels great and can help grow your business, but if your unpaid commitments diminish the level of service to paying customers, it's not helping anyone.

Also, avoid out of pocket expenses. You're volunteering your time and expertise, not your wallet. Whenever possible, discuss out of pocket expenses in advance to determine the appropriate person within the organization to coordinate with for reimbursement.

Finally, limit volunteer work to a pre-determined number of events per year, with many opting for between one-two bigger events or three-four smaller events, depending on the time said events require.

You can post a promo video on your website or on social media. When it comes to marketing, don't put all your eggs in a single basket. Most of the time, it's not enough to market solely through paid advertisements or on social media. Spread out your marketing efforts and track them.

If you're expending time or resources, it's important to know what you're getting in return. If you're spending money each month on a radio ad that isn't bringing in new clients, you're wasting money.

Likewise, if you're donating your time planning a charity event or curating your Insta feed, but it's not leading to new leads, you're wasting your time.

Track the amount of time and money you spend on each marketing tactic, the number of leads it generates, and how much actual business you get from it throughout the year, then analyze the results.

Some efforts require more time than others to generate actual business. So don't expect instant results with everything, but try to get an idea of the turn around time for each initiative you undertake and analyze it accordingly on a monthly, quarterly, or annual basis.

Once you have an idea of what marketing tactics bring in the most business, make a plan to allot more resources to them in the following quarter or year, then analyze if the additional time or money reaped a greater benefit.

Finally, remember marketing isn't static; what works changes over time. You may discover your social media initiative paid off great in year one but isn't getting the same results in year three. When that happens, it's time to shake things up. Try a new approach or allocate more resources towards other initiatives.

In marketing, it's about determining what works now, in your local area, with your ideal customer base.

Public Relations

As a local business owner and area professional, it never hurts to build a strong relationship with the local media. The goals of this are three-fold.

The first goal is to get coverage of your business and generate media response when you send out a press release. Reporters are inundated with press releases on a daily basis. So in order to get media attention, both your release and your name need to stand out.

Reporters prefer properly formatted, informative releases, written in AP style, with the most important facts in bold at the top. Always include your contact information and any other contact information central to coverage of the event in bold at the bottom of the release.

When writing your release, including who, what, when, and where in the first paragraph of the release, but keep it short, if you can't answer all those things in less than 65 words, break it up into two short paragraphs at the top of the release.

Some newspapers and magazines allow reporters to write short blurbs or mini-articles on press releases alone, so it's a good idea to include quotes from one or more sources. Make sure all quotes are attributed to someone and include the person's first and last name, age (if applicable) and title or area of expertise.

The idea isn't to overwhelm them with junk, rather provide everything they need to get a feel for what you're doing and the information they would include in an article, should they write one.

The second goal is to become their go-to expert on food trucks. If they're writing a lifestyle piece on the food truck scene in the area, they're going to need sources, and you want them to think of you.

This not only helps establish your expertise with the local community, but it also gets your name out there and in front of potential clients.

The third goal is for them to come to you directly and treat you fairly, should something occur to ever cause an uproar or result in harm, damage, or tragedy.

In these instances, the last thing you may want is public attention, but how you handle unfortunate circumstances can have a permanent impact on your image in the community. It's better to set the tone and get the facts out there than to let someone else do it for you.

Working With Reporters

Reporters tend to turn a nose at anything that reeks of sales. If they opt to cover an event you're participating in, it's because they genuinely think it provides important or useful information, or it will make for interesting reading.

If it's a community fluff piece and they have to work, hounding a minimum number of sources and trying to figure out visually appealing art to run with it, it's hardly worth the hassle.

Try to give them everything they need to write an article in an afternoon. That includes all the details, quotes, access to sources, and whenever possible, compelling art to run with it. Relationship building is key to having good connections in media.

Follow the work of a few reporters that cover business, local events, or the like. Read their articles. When you read a particularly well-written piece, reach out to them to let them know you enjoyed it.

After you worked with a reporter, send a thank you email letting them know you appreciated their coverage of the event, add them to your annual holiday or birthday card list, and reach out from time to time to keep the connection strong.

Chapter 10: Mistakes to Avoid

So now you should have the knowledge and confidence to get your new food truck underway. But, not so fast! There are a few pitfalls that first-time small business owners find themselves falling into.

Not knowing their competition.

Is your food truck competing against just other food trucks, or are you also competing against local food trucks that offer catering services or have a mobile unit? You should be sure to do extensive research about what options your customers have. Hopefully, you conducted this research when you were trying to come up with a name and menu and deciding who your ideal customer would be. You should be filling a need in your community with your new food truck. Do something the others are not doing!

Having a bad digital presence.

You MUST have and use social media on more than one platform. You also must have a website, so you are searchable online. Connect your social media to your website. You may even want to consider blogging or adding regular updates about your business. Pay attention to online reviews. Ask for feedback and act on it.

Budgeting wrongly.

Be realistic. Plan for what cannot be foreseen. Have an emergency fund. Bad budgeting can suck the life out of your business.

Inconsistent branding.

Come up with a name, logo, theme, and catchphrase for your business. Use this same imagery everywhere, in every single place that your business has a presence. Being a food truck, someone should be able to look at your truck or hear your name and know what you do immediately.

Going it alone.

You can't run a food truck by yourself. Solicit the help of friends, professionals, and others who share your vision.

You clearly cannot cook the food alone, why would you try to run things all by yourself? Most managers also need an assistant manager. Head chefs need a sous chef. Again, people get accounting and legal degrees for a reason!

Appendix: Food Truck Events

I took a minute to survey the activities and events surrounding the location I would place my food truck. There are a slew of things to participant in for free or maybe a small nominal fee.

But this is chump change compared to the value in creating awareness about your food truck for future customers who may come on board with you, and you just might make some money by selling some of your food items to others who are attending. This is a win-win situation, hands down.

These are the events to explore potential opportunities before they occur. If nothing else, you just might meet new friends or an alliance to network with or share concerns to boot.

Are you considering attending a food truck festival this year? There can be one happening right in your backyard which you weren't even aware of.

I have compiled a list of the most important food truck festivals across the nation. Whether or not you're a seasoned food truck owner or thinking about stepping into the business, these events may be pretty enlightening.

Ultimately, these kinds of events give the possibility of satisfying and hooking up with different folks inside the industry.

Columbus Food Truck Festival – Columbus, Ohio

Chicago Food Truck Festival – Chicago, Illinois

L.A. Street Food Fest - Los Angeles, California

Atlanta Street Food Festival – Atlanta, Georgia

Seattle Street Food Festival – Seattle, Washington

Sea Isle City Food Truck Fest – New Jersey

Main Street Food Truck Festival – Little Rock, Arkansas

Street Eats Food Truck Festival - Scottsdale, Arizona

Eat the Street - Oahu, Hawaii

Taste of Three Cities - Baltimore, Washington, D.C., and Philadelphia

The Great Texas Food Truck Rally – Dallas, Texas

H & 8th Night Market – Oklahoma City, Oklahoma

Tampa Bay Food Truck Rally – Tampa, Florida

The World's Largest Food Truck Rally – St. Petersburg, Florida

Conclusion

The fastest growing industry in the world is the food truck sector. In fact, many people are turning to food trucks with a catering component. Customers are enjoying the convenience of eating a wide variety of meals at low-cost with gourmet food options.

In 2008, with the economic downturn, people were losing their jobs and had to look to other avenues for employment where food trucks gained upward visibility in the marketplace. Cities like New York, Gordonsville, Austin, and Atlanta show food trucks in nearly every neighborhood. Investing in a food truck business can be lucrative but still risky. It's important to do your homework and research trends before making that move.

The gourmet segment of the food industry has shown a rapid rise over the last few years. Food trucks fill a void in preparing quick, tasty lunches, breakfasts, and dinners on the go. The only reserve in opening your food truck enterprise is the sometimes-lengthy licensures and permits requirements. Laws typically regulate the distance in that it can't operate too closely to a food truck.

Food trucks and other eateries are lobbying to curb the growth in the food truck industry and to thwart the competition. Maybe changes in the way food truck operators band together will create innovations in the industry.

Thank you for reading this book. I wish you the very best in starting your new enterprise!

If this book
has helped you in any way,
please consider
leaving a review
whereever you
purchased this book.
Thank you!

Made in the USA
Middletown, DE
01 May 2021